THE NUCLEAR CASEBOOK
—An Illustrated Guide—

by Dr. C. Phillips and Dr. I. Ross

Polygon Books

First published 1983 by
Polygon Books,
1 Buccleuch Place, Edinburgh, EH8 9LW.

Copyright © 1983 C. PHILLIPS and I. ROSS.

Typeset by EUSPB.

Printed by McQueen Printers, Galashiels from artwork supplied.

ISBN 0 904919 71 4

Acknowledgments

This book has been very much a collaborative effort.
Cover design: Jenny Phillips based on 'The False Mirror' by Rene Magritte.
Art Work: Jenny Phillips and David Simon.
Cartoonists: Raymond Briggs and Mel Calman.
Word Processing by hand: Mrs P. Hunter and C. A. Mackenzie *et al*.
The Friendly Ear; Neville Moir of Polygon Books.
MCANW: For the original literature search on the medical effects: Dr Frank Boulton, Dr Christine Dean, Dr Nigel Hurst, Professor J. R. S. Fincham, Dr Ken Jones, Dr Christopher Ludlam, Dr Ian McCarthy, Dr Judith McDonald, Dr Shirley Ratcliffe, Dr Maureen Roberts, Dr Brian Venters, and Dr Helen Zeally.
For critical reading of the text, Margaret Fraser, Dr Shirley Ratcliffe, Dr Nigel Hurst, Andrea Joyce.
IPPNW: Professor Robert Jay Lifton and Dr K. Erikson.
SANA: Dr Alan Longman, Professor Michael Pentz, Dr Assam Quisrawi, Dr Philip Steadman, David Simmonds, Stuart Swanson and Alan Walker.
Others: Dr Hector Cameron, Nigel Mace and Duncan Campbell and his public spirited moles.
We would also like to thank: Wildwood House Ltd for the use of pictures from *Unforgettable Fire*; Hamish Hamilton Ltd for the use of cartoons from Raymond Briggs' *When The Wind Blows*; Research Institute for Nuclear Medicine and Biology, Hiroshima University for the photograph of a man dying from Radiation Sickness; Shogo Yamahata for the Hiroshima photographs on pages 5 and 44 taken by his Father Yosuke Yamahata; Professor G. Melvyn Howe for the use of smallpox photograph.

For Anna and Barnaby
and all the other children born into this World.

Contents

Introduction

During the 1981 Edinburgh International Festival the Medical Campaign Against Nuclear Weapons (MCANW) mounted an exhibition illustrating the medical effects of nuclear war. Subsequently, many requests were made for copies of this exhibition and it was felt that it would be helpful to have a book which people could take home to read at leisure. In producing this book however, we have added a great deal of new material and so we hope that it will be useful whether or not the exhibition has been seen.

When we began work on the 1981 exhibition we started from a position of relative ignorance, but rapidly came to realise that nuclear weapons produce destruction and loss of life on a scale which is hard to comprehend and to which there could be no effective medical response. This conclusion is confirmed in the 1983 BMA report —

The explosion of a single nuclear bomb of the size used at Hiroshima over a major city in the UK is likely to produce so many cases of trauma and burns requiring hospital treatment that the remaining medical services in the UK would be completely overwhelmed[1].

Many people still adhere to the belief that nuclear war can only be prevented by continuing to deploy newer and more sophisticated weapons. We, and others, believe this is a tragic misconception of the real nature of the arms race. During the last decade there have been many technological advances, particularly in the field of missile accuracy, and many impartial analysts believe that these innovations are undermining the security and stability that was believed to result from nuclear deterrence. An understanding of these factors is crucial to the whole debate and so are dealt with in some depth (pp 10-21). We have also given considerable space to illustrate the work of Oppenshaw and Steadman (Scientists Against Nuclear Weapons — SANA) who were the first to undertake a detailed investigation of discrepancies in the Home Office's estimates for casualties following a nuclear attack. While this section does not address the fundamental question as to how we can prevent nuclear war it does throw doubt on the integrity of some official statements.

Since these weapons have potentially indiscriminate effects on defenceless civilians many feel that even their threatened use can never be justified. None the less there seems to be good evidence to suggest that recent developments have made a mockery of the concept of nuclear deterrence and that present policies are leading down a road to destruction.

However you the reader must examine the evidence we present and draw your own conclusions.

We are greatly indebted to all those who have helped directly or indirectly to produce this book and a full list of acknowledgements appears on the title page. Any errors or omissions are our responsibility.

Crispin Phillips, B.Sc., Ph.D.
Molecular Biologist
Research Associate at the
Centre for Human Ecology —
University of Edinburgh.

Ian R. F. Ross, M.B.Ch.B.
General Medical Practitioner,
Part-time Lecturer In General Practice,
University of Edinburgh.

Edinburgh — May 1983.

Human history has been interspersed by wars, and for many centuries war has been accepted as an ultimate means, legitimate or otherwise, of resolving major differences between nations.

Following the Napoleonic Wars the Prussian strategist, Carl von Clausewitz, wrote a treatise "On War",[2] a work which is still considered relevant in military circles. Clausewitz saw war as a rational instrument of national policy. However, Clausewitz lived at a time when armies were relatively small and their destructive power was limited.

By 1900 the potential for destruction had increased greatly and as a result, the Hague Convention of 1907 attempted to set limits to war in order to spare civilian populations and limit destruction. Although the Convention was essentially honoured in the 1914-18 War,[3] the indiscriminate bombing of cities and civilian populations by both sides during the Second World War was clearly in breach of the 1907 Hague Convention. Such bombing could only be achieved by major military operations — for example Dresden was devastated in February 1945 by bombs from 1,083 aircraft.[4]

In contrast on Monday, 6th August 1945, a single B-29 bomber dropped one atom bomb and destroyed a whole city — Hiroshima. War had become unlimited and potentially unlimitable.

Kizo Kawakami age 71

Masato Yamashita age 52

August 9
  With no one to help her, a girl died leaning on the bank of the Enko River.

The following reproductions are from paintings by Hiroshima Survivors 30 years after the event. The full collection of paintings can be seen in *Unforgettable Fire*, published originally by Nippon Hoso Shuppan Kyokai, Tokyo, (and in Britain by:- Wildwood House, Ltd., Gloucester Mansions, Cambridge Circus, London).

6

turning point

Name unknown, housewife

At Meiji Bridge

A mother, driven half-mad, while looking for her child, was calling his name. At last she found him. His head looked like a boiled octopus. His eyes were half-closed, and his mouth was white, pursed, and swollen.

Kazuo Matsumuro died in 1977.

On the stairs in front of the statue of Fleet Admiral Kato in Hijiyama Park.

Although we were lying side by side we did not recognise each other. He heard my voice and said, "Are you Mr Matsumuro?" It was Mr Yoshimoto. His face was dark and swollen. He seemed unable to open his eyes or mouth. The left side of his face, neck, and hands were burned. Soon we were separated.

I was bleeding from my ears, nose, and mouth and was wounded from being crushed. I learned later that the twelfth backbone and the first lumbar vertebra were fractured. I could hardly move.

7

Civilian and Military Casualties

European

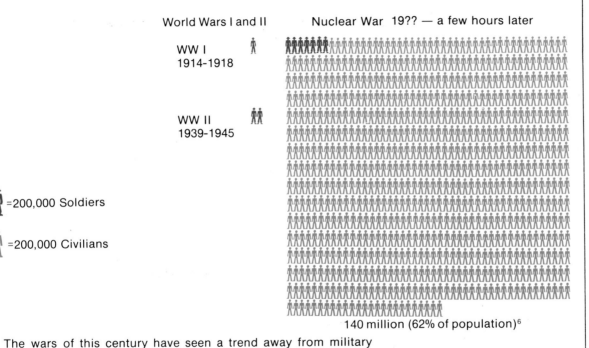

World Wars I and II

WW I
1914-1918

WW II
1939-1945

Nuclear War 19?? — a few hours later

140 million (62% of population)[6]

World Wars I and II

WW I

WW II

=200,000 Soldiers

=200,000 Civilians

The wars of this century have seen a trend away from military casualties towards civilian casualties. The ratio of military to civilian deaths were:[8]

World War 1 20:1 (ie 20 military deaths for 1 civilian death)
World War 2 1:1
Korea   1:5
Vietnam   1:20
Nuclear War 1:100+

In a nuclear war the majority of civilians will be casualties[6] [7]. Therefore, it is vital for each of us to have a clear understanding of the policies upon which our lives depend.

in Twentieth Century Wars

War Deaths[5] [7] [8]

Nuclear War

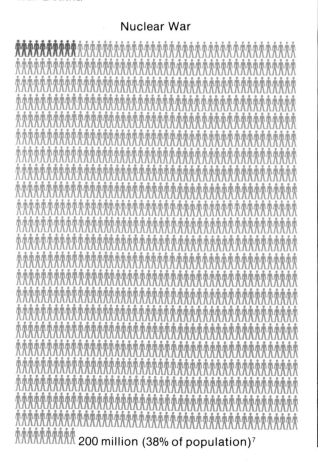

200 million (38% of population)[7]

Soviet War Deaths [5] [6] [8]

World Wars I and II

Nuclear War

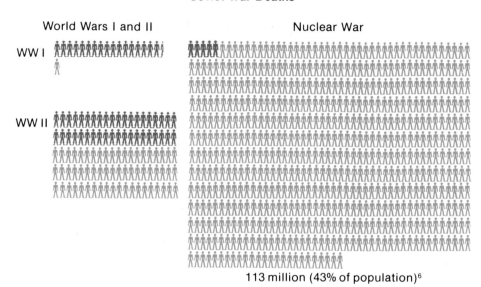

WW I

WW II

113 million (43% of population)[6]

Nowhere is the bitter experience of the last war felt more keenly
than in the Soviet Union.
Soviet Union[5] [8] lost 1 person in 8.
Britain[5] lost 1 person in 130
United States[5] lost 1 person in 325.

Diminishing returns in absurdity

Destruction and Weapon Yield

A 1 kiloton nuclear bomb releases the explosive energy of a thousand (1000) tons of TNT.
A 1 megaton nuclear bomb releases the explosive energy of a million (1,000,000) tons of TNT.

However, it should be realised that the amount of damage caused by a nuclear weapon does not increase in direct proportion to its explosive power. This is a consequence of "volume geometry".

For example, a 1 megaton bomb divided into ten smaller 100 kiloton bombs would cause blast damage twice that of the original 1 megaton bomb.

The Destruction of Deterrence

On August 6th 1945, the 12.5 kiloton nuclear bomb which was dropped on Hiroshima killed between 78,000 and 100,000[10].

'little boy'

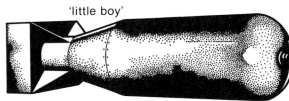

Today the combined arsenals of both superpowers are in excess of sixteen thousand megatons, equivalent to nearly 1.5 million Hiroshima bombs[11][12]. However, when the size of the various bombs are taken into account, the destructive power is somewhat less and equivalent to just over three hundred thousand Hiroshima bombs. This is illustrated on the opposite page.

In an industrialised country a large proportion of the population live in cities and large towns[9][13]. The use of nuclear weapons make the destruction of these population centres relatively easy. However, as the targets become smaller and more numerous, such as towns and villages, so more and more weapons are required for their destruction, but with less and less effect. This point was made clear in a Pentagon study carried out in the 1960's which found that maximum levels of destruction to the Soviet Union could be achieved with about 400 megatons and thereafter the damage inflicted by further bombs had little impact (see graph)[14].

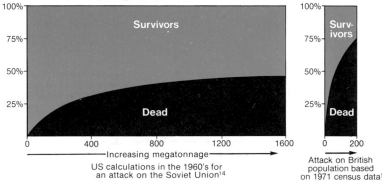

US calculations in the 1960's for an attack on the Soviet Union[14]

Attack on British population based on 1971 census data[15]

The possession today of 16,000 megatons by the superpowers is thus greatly in excess of that required for deterrence. What is the purpose of this vast destructive power? The answer is that our strategy of nuclear deterrence based on the threat of unacceptable damage has been replaced by a new strategy known as COUNTER FORCE.

	Strategic[11][12] Nuclear Weapons		Theatre & Tactical[11] Nuclear Weapons		Total Arsenal	
1982	Number of Warheads	Megatons	Number of Warheads	Megatons	Number of Warheads	Megatons
USA	9,500	3,500	14,343	5,300	23,843	8,800
USSR	8,800	4,500	5,763	3,100	12,420	7,600

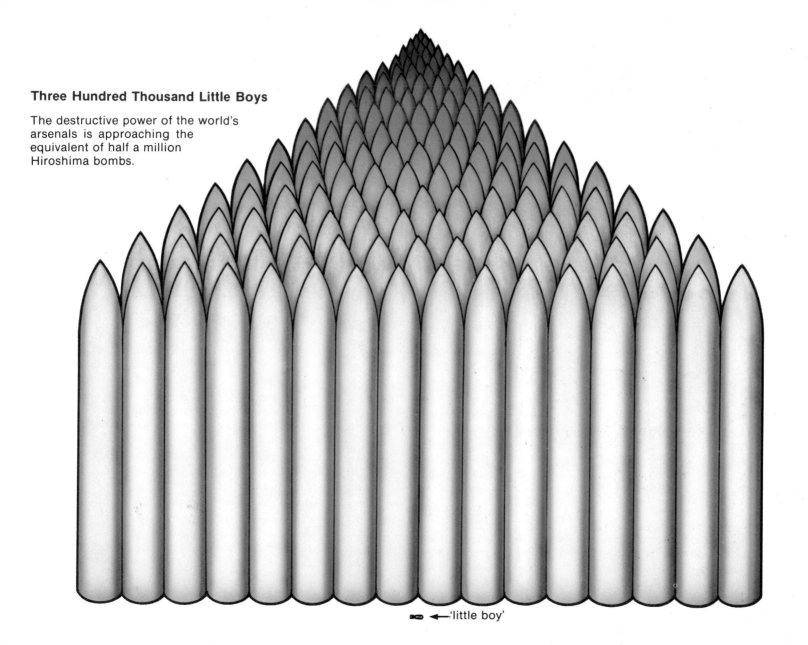

Three Hundred Thousand Little Boys

The destructive power of the world's arsenals is approaching the equivalent of half a million Hiroshima bombs.

◄— 'little boy'

Evolution of Weapons

Since the early 1960's nuclear deterrence has been based on the concept of Mutually Assured Destruction (MAD). Both super-powers realised that although each could launch a devastating attack neither side could destroy the others ability to retaliate in an equally devastating manner. The stability and security of MAD depended therefore upon two factors:

 i) The ability to destroy each others cities;
 ii) The inability to destroy each others missiles.

However, the development of COUNTERFORCE STRATEGY, which depends upon being able to destroy the other sides missiles in their silos, has undermined the very essence of the MAD doctrine and made nuclear war more likely. The importance of missile accuracy for the implementation of COUNTERFORCE STRATEGY[16] is illustrated on this page.

Destruction of a hardened missile silo depends more upon warhead accuracy than upon megatonnage.

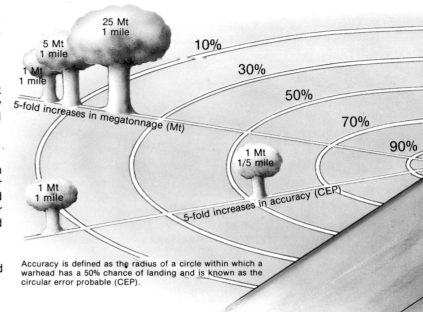

Accuracy is defined as the radius of a circle within which a warhead has a 50% chance of landing and is known as the circular error probable (CEP).

EVOLUTION OF SOVIET WEAPONS

	SSN5 (SLBM)	SS 8 (ICBM)	SS 9 (ICBM)	SSN 8 (SLBM)	SS 19 (ICBM)	SS 17 (ICBM)	SSN 18 (SLBM)	SS 18 mod 4 (ICBM)	SSNX20 (SLBM)	NEW (ICBM)	SS20 (IMRBM)
SLBM Submarine launched ballistic missile											
ICBM Inter continental ballistic missile											
IMRBM Intermediate range ballistic missile											
ACLM Air launched Cruise missile											
Date of deployment	1963	1963	1966	1973	1976	1977	1977	1979	1983		1977
Range in nautical miles	700	6,000	6500	4300	5000	5400	4050	5500	4500		2700
Number of warheads	1×Mt	1×5 Mt	1×20 Mt	1×1 Mt	6×0.5 Mt	4×0.5 Mt	3×0.2 Mt	10×0.5 Mt	....	?	3×15 Mt
Accuracy (CEP)	1½ miles	1 mile	¾ mile	½ mile	1500 ft	1200 ft	½ mile	950 ft	....		1320 ft
Probability of destroying hardened target	1%	3%	37%	11%	26%	39%	3%	50%	....		10%

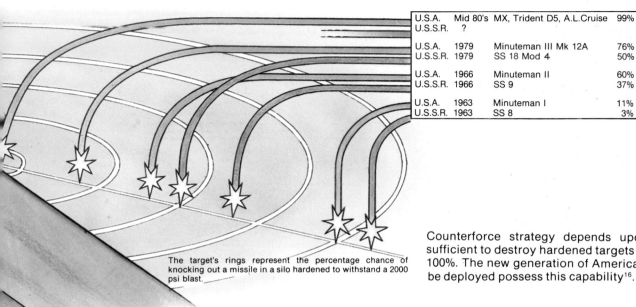

U.S.A.	Mid 80's	MX, Trident D5, A.L.Cruise	99%
U.S.S.R.	?		
U.S.A.	1979	Minuteman III Mk 12A	76%
U.S.S.R.	1979	SS 18 Mod 4	50%
U.S.A.	1966	Minuteman II	60%
U.S.S.R.	1966	SS 9	37%
U.S.A.	1963	Minuteman I	11%
U.S.S.R.	1963	SS 8	3%

The target's rings represent the percentage chance of knocking out a missile in a silo hardened to withstand a 2000 psi blast.

Counterforce strategy depends upon weapons with accuracies sufficient to destroy hardened targets with a probability approaching 100%. The new generation of American weapons which are about to be deployed possess this capability[16].

EVOLUTION OF AMERICAN WEAPONS [19] [20]

Pershing II (IMRBM)	MX (ICBM)	Trident D5 (SLBM)	Air launched Cruise missile (ALCM)	Minuteman III Mk 12A (ICBM)	Trident C4 (SLBM)	Minuteman III (ICBM)	Poseidon C3 (SLBM)	Minuteman II (ICBM)	Polaris A3 (SLBM)	Minuteman I (ICBM)	Titan II (ICBM)	Polaris A1 (SLBM)
1983	Mid 80's	Mid 80's	1983	1979	1979	1970	1970	1966	1964	1963	1962	1960
970	6000	6000	1350	7000	4000	7000	2500	7000	2500	6500	6300	1200
×0.25 Mt	14×0.35/0.5Mt	7×0.475 Mt	1×0.2 Mt	3×0.35 Mt	8×0.1 Mt	3×0.17 Mt	10×0.04 Mt	1×1.5 Mt	3×0.2 Mt	1×1 Mt	1 x 9 Mt	1×1 Mt
100 ft	300 ft	400 ft	200 ft	650 ft	1600 ft	980 ft	1700 ft	1300 ft	½ mile	½ mile	¾ mile	1 mile
100%	99%	99%	100%	76%	10%	30%	6%	60%	5%	11%	23%	3%

Counterforce strategy, which threatens enemy hardened targets such as missile silos, requires the ability to deliver nuclear warheads with great accuracy. The strategy also requires missiles with multiple independently targetable warheads.

e.g. Suppose each side had 100 missiles each with a single warhead. A successful counterforce attack would require that each warhead explodes on target destroying all of the enemies missiles, for otherwise the enemy could retaliate with any remaining missiles.

If however, each side had 100 missiles, each with 10 independently targetable warheads, then one side could launch a counterforce attack using only half of its missiles. In such an attack involving 500 warheads, each of the enemy's missiles would be targeted with 5 warheads thus increasing the probability of their destruction. Even if a few of the enemy's missiles were not destroyed the attacker would still have unused missiles targeted on the enemy's cities to deter retaliation.

USSR			
Year	Strategic* Lethality	Major Weapon	Contribution of major weapon to Lethality
1965	1,037	SS9	61%
1970	6,037	SS9	71%
1975	7,094	SS9	61%
1980	42,284	SS18 & 19	41 & 42%
1985	??,???	SS18 & 19	?? & ??%

The two tables show that increases in lethality are principally brought about by the deployment of new types of weapons.

* Bombers are not included in the lethality calculation because they are slow and vunerable to air defence.

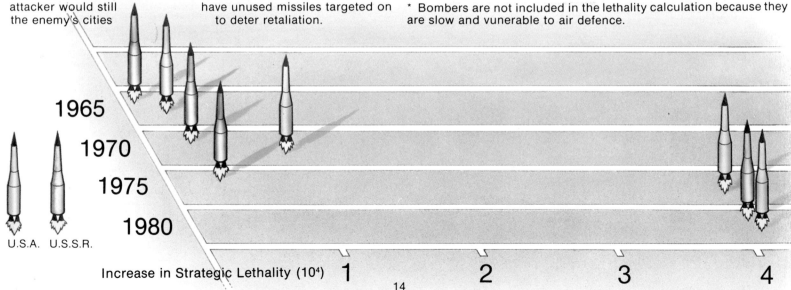

1965
1970
1975
1980

U.S.A. U.S.S.R.

Increase in Strategic Lethality (10^4)   1   2   3   4

USA			
Year	Strategic* Lethality	Major Weapon	Contribution of major weapon to Lethality
1965	4,716	Minuteman I	68%
1970	19,375	Minuteman II	77%
1975	41,520	Minuteman III	47%
1980	43,549	Minuteman III	45%
1985	833,450	Cruise (ALCM)	90%

A measure of counterforce capability is the LETHALITY of the strategic arsenals which takes into account not only the number and yield of the nuclear warheads on ballistic* missiles but also their accuracy.

The illustration on the opposite page shows the lethality of the superpowers strategic arsenals at five year intervals from 1965 to 1980, (also see tables). The illustration at the bottom of this page shows the dramatic increase in lethality of the US strategic arsenal as a result of deploying cruise missiles (note increase in scale).

It can be argued that since cruise missiles are relatively slow they are not weapons of surprise, essential for a counterforce strategy. However because of their long range and invisibility to air defences they have been included in the lethality calculation for 1985. From 1985 onward the US plan to deploy MX and trident D5 ballistic missiles whose accuracies approach that of cruise missiles.

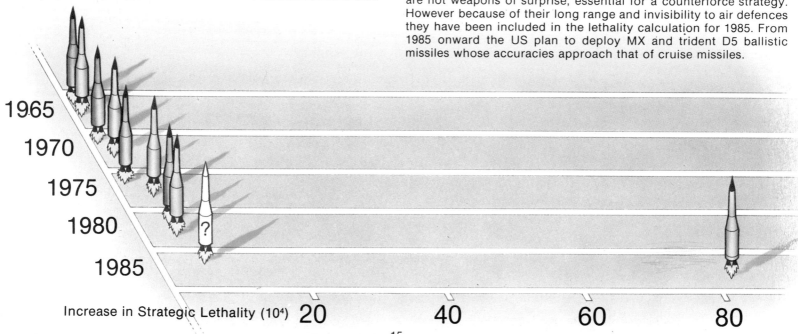

1965
1970
1975
1980
1985

Increase in Strategic Lethality (10^4) 20 40 60 80

Counterforce strategy and the erosion of deterrence

The doctrine of MUTUALLY ASSURED DESTRUCTION (MAD) arose as a result of the deployment in the 1960's of nuclear ballistic missiles against which neither side had any effective defence.

The MAD doctrine reflected the available technology; thus Intercontinental Ballistic Missiles (ICBM) were only accurate enough to destroy large targets such as cities, and smaller targents such as missile silos were relatively safe. This situation was stable, even in times of crisis, because although each superpower had the ability to destroy the other's cities it was deterred from this as it would inevitably have led to the destruction of its own cities. The development of very accurate warheads which can destroy the other side's missiles in their silos has given rise to a strategy called COUNTERFORCE which renders deterrence obsolete.

In addition to accuracy the other component of a COUNTER-FORCE strategy is the possession of missiles with multiple warheads which are independently targetable.

The large increase in the number of nuclear warheads (shown on pp 18-19) is partly due to the deployment of new missiles during the 60's and 70's but mainly due to their conversion to multiple warheads reflecting the implementation of counterforce strategy. Counterforce strategy was first made public in 1974 in a Congressional Hearing by US Defence Secretary Schlesinger and the doctrine was affirmed by Carter in his Presidential Directive 59 (1980).

USA leads the way

The USA has always had a considerable lead in counterforce capability (pp 13-15). In 1970 the US deployed the Minuteman III which was the first ICBM to have multiple independently targetable warheads. In addition these missiles could deliver their warheads with greater accuracy than before (CEP 980 ft)[14]. It was another five years (1975) before the USSR could deploy an ICBM with multiple independently targetable warheads — the SS19. However the accuracy of these warheads (CEP 1500 ft) was no better than the ten year old US Minuteman II (CEP 1300 ft)[19].

Today while the USSR are deploying the present generation of strategic nuclear weapons the US are about to leave the Soviets far behind by deploying the next generation of counterforce weapons (pp 12-15).

COUNTERFORCE JUSTIFIED

Counterforce — a psychological strategy

The justification of counterforce strategy by the US Defence Department is interesting. It is argued that if the USSR launched a first strike against US missile silos they would keep back a significant proportion of their silo based missiles to be targeted on US cities so as to deter retaliation. Therefore, for the US to retaliate against Soviet cities as demanded by the MAD doctrine, it would be necessary to destroy those silo based missiles. This was called "Second Strike Counterforce Capability" by the Defence Department. The destabilising nature of this strategy was emphasised in a 1978 Congressional Budget Office background paper[21]:

. . . There may be an inescapable dilemma in the procurement of second strike counterforce capability: a US arsenal large enough to attack Soviet ICBMs after having absorbed a first strike would be large enough to threaten the Soviet ICBM force in a US first strike. Moreover, the Soviet Union looking at capabilities rather than intentions, might see a US second-strike capability in this light. Faced with a threat to their ICBM force, Soviet leaders facing an international crisis might have an incentive to use their missiles in a pre-emptive all out strike before they could be destroyed by the United States.

# of Strategy

Counterforce — a military strategy

One justification for adopting a counterforce strategy was the belief that the MAD doctrine was not a credible deterrent in protecting vital US interests. The Soviets might consider that a conventional war in Europe or the Middle East whatever the outcome would not become nuclear because of the fear of mutual destruction[22].

Counterforce strategy lowers the threshold for a nuclear war by threatening the enemy's ability to retaliate. In times of crisis each side will be frightened that the other side will be the first to launch a debilitating counterforce attack. The pressure to strike first will therefore be enormous.

Paradoxically, it is this lowering of the nuclear threshold that is thought by some to raise the credibility of nuclear deterrence and therefore our security[23]. The lowering of the nuclear threshold is also the basis of the NATO strategy of flexible response and first use of nuclear weapons[24] but in this case it has been achieved by integrating battlefield and theatre nuclear weapons with conventional forces.

Thus, to the risk of a
nuclear war by accident has been added
nuclear war by misperception (counterforce strategy) and
nuclear war by escalation (NATO flexible response).

Counterforce — an economic strategy

Another explanation for the development of a counterforce strategy, with its inherent risks, is that the US is attempting to break the Soviet economy. Although both superpowers spend approximately the same total amount on their defence, this is twice the burden for the Soviet Union because their GNP (economic wealth) is half that of the USA[9][25]. The recently publicised Pentagon document "Fiscal Year 1984-1988 Defence Guidance"[26] supports this economic argument. It asserts:

that the US and its allies should in peacetime declare economic and technological war on the Soviet Union . . . that the US should develop weapons for the Soviets to counter, impose disproportionate costs, open up new areas of major military competition and obsolesce previous Soviet investment.

This economic argument may be one of the reasons for deploying Cruise missiles. Although Cruise missiles are highly accurate, their advocates point out that they are too slow to be counterforce weapons. However because they have a small radar image (no bigger than a seagull) and fly very low they will be extremely difficult for the Soviets to detect with their present radar systems. To prevent a surprise attack the Soviets will be forced to deploy aircraft along their borders equipped with "look-down" radar at an estimated cost of over £35,000 million.[27]

Economic war is potentially dangerous and it should be remembered that the economic collapse of Germany brought about by reparations to France was one factor which facilitated Hitler's rise to power[28]. Intense economic pressure may therefore produce unpredictable effects.

Counterforce — a strategy of the military/industrial complex

Many consider that the enemy of democracy lies as much within our borders as without. President Eisenhower's warning of the power of the military-industrial complex created by the needs of World War II were well justified. There is considerable evidence to suggest that the economic and political vested interests of the military-industrial complex contributes more to the momentum of the arms race than does the threat of Soviet domination[29].

In both the USA and USSR there are less than 200 cities and towns with populations of over 150,000. The 400 pin heads on the map represent nuclear explosions on these centres resulting in the death of 1/3 of the entire population of each country — more than enough for deterrence.

Effective air defence against bombers meant that Mutual Destruction was not assured.

It was the advent of ballistic missiles against which there was no defence that gave rise to the doctrine of Mutually Assured Destruction (most people's idea of deterrence). By 1961 the USA could deliver 200 warheads by ballistic missiles. By 1964 the USSR could do likewise.

1960's

The 16,000 pin heads on the map, represent random explosions of the total number of strategic (intercontinental) nuclear warheads possessed by the USA and the USSR in 1981.[23]

The SALT II Agreement of Vienna 1979 (unratified by the USA) allows the combined number of stratetic nuclear warheads to increase to well over 20,000 by 1985 when the treaty expires.[19]

If as well as strategic, theatre and tactical nuclear warheads are taken into the account then the number of pin heads on the map can be doubled.[11]

The radius of the pin heads is 10 miles on the map scale. The shock wave of a 1 megaton airburst would cause extensive damage to domestic buildings 10 miles from detonation.

1980's

Deterrence Policy

Based on the threat of being able to retaliate after an attack with such devastating effect that a potential aggressor is deterred from attacking.

For deterrence to be effective, the ability to retaliate must survive the initial attack. Hence the heavy reliance on submarine-launched missiles and hardened silos for land-based missiles.

For both the USA and USSR the possession of 400-600 nuclear weapons would give each the potential to destroy $1/3$-$1/2$ of the other's population — more than sufficient for effective deterrence.

Counterforce Strategy

Based on the stringent requirement of destroying the enemy's weapons quickly, efficiently and WITHOUT WARNING.

This means a LARGE NUMBER of offensive weapons which can approach their targets without detection. It also means HIGHLY ACCURATE and reliable weapons which guarantee destroying the enemy's weapons before they can be launched.

In both the USA and USSR the patterns of technological progress over the past decade show a deliberate development of counterforce capability.

The defensive posture of each side to counterforce strategy is to have their weapons ready to be launched on warning (like a gun with the safety catch off).

As 'launch on warning' relies heavily on computers, the chance of technical failure resulting in false alarms makes an accidental war ever more likely.

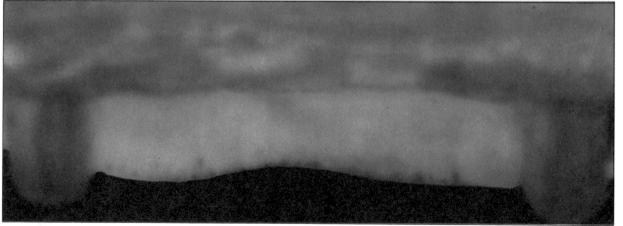

Medical Effects

IMMEDIATE EFFECTS

Nuclear explosions produce heat, blast and radiation. Heat and blast give rise to burns and trauma.

Trauma:

Caused by collapse of buildings, flying debris and direct blast effects. Typical examples are shown:

Severe leg injury

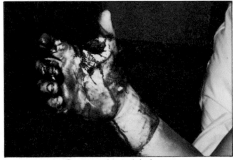
Severe hand injury

Burns:

Caused by direct heat flash and indirectly by burning materials. These are often complicated by toxic smoke (which is often produced by modern furniture) and/or flame inhalation.

Child with severe body burns

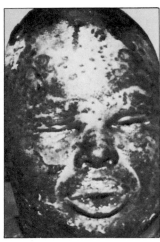
Flash burns to face (Hiroshima)

These types of injuries require prompt treatment and may take weeks or months of intensive care and reconstructive surgery.

A one megaton explosion over a city would produce many thousands of such injured persons and overwhelm the medical capacity of the developed world. In the whole of the UK there are only 106 beds specifically assigned for serious burns cases[1].

# of Nuclear War

DELAYED EFFECTS

Radiation sickness:

Radioactivity kills dividing cells. This affects primarily the gut lining and the blood forming cells and can result in uncontrollable diarrhoea, vomiting, internal bleeding, massive infection, coma and death within hours, days or weeks. Survivors may never fully recover.

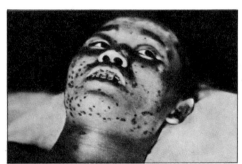

A young man dying of radiation sickness.
Facial spots due to subcutaneous bleeding (Hiroshima).

Photograph: Kimura Gonichi from U.S. Army returned material courtesy of Research Institute for Nuclear Medicine and Biology Hiroshima University.

You cannot detect lethal radiation without sophisticated instruments. You will therefore not know whether you are being exposed.

Infectious diseases:

Insanitary conditions from thousands of rotting corpses, flies, and vermin together with lowered resistance from radiation and malnutrition provide the best possible conditions for uncontrollable infectious diseases. These will include hepatitis, dysentry, tuberculosis, cholera, typhoid fever and typhus[30] [31]. Many of these are fatal without intensive medical treatment.

Smallpox (Glasgow 1920)

In 1967 it was estimated that 10 million people suffered from smallpox of whom 2 million died.

It took 12 years of international co-operation before the World Health Organisation could declare that in 1980 Smallpox had been eradicated[32]. This achievement cost 300 million dollars, the equivalent of the cost of 2.5 days of the nuclear arms race.

LONG TERM EFFECTS

Cancer:

Increased environmental radiation will cause an increase in cancer. For example, the incidence of leukaemia increased in Japanese survivors, especially in children.

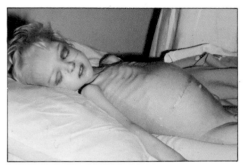

Cancer

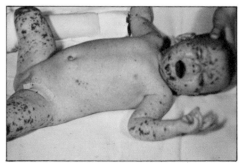

Leukaemia

Birth Defects:

Radiation causes genetic mutations; these can result in birth defects. Following a full scale nuclear war we can expect many more abnormal babies.

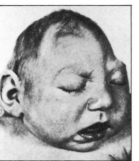

Microcephaly

Malnutrition:

Our diet depends upon agriculture, trade, industry and transport. These will be largely destroyed, together with the skills inherent in their operation. Starvation will become a permanent aspect of life as it is in poorer countries[31]. Deficiency diseases such as rickets, kwashiorkor, beri-beri and scurvy are likely. Infant mortality would inevitably increase.

Infertility:

Irradiation of the reproductive organs can cause sterility.

Modern medical facilities, which are the product of centuries of development, cannot be recreated easily. The knowledge and pool of skills that we have acquired will be irretrievably lost and our resources destroyed. The only effective medical response to nuclear war is prevention.

The Wind of Change

Following a Nuclear Attack, 50% of deaths could result from fallout radiation. (BMA Report — 1983).[1]

In a Nuclear War it is likely that many victims will suffer from the combined effects of radiation, burns, and blast. Consequently, injuries which may be relatively minor under normal circumstances could be fatal when combined with others of similar severity, particularly in the absence of adequate treatment and basic sanitation. (BMA Report — 1983)

Most Doctors and other Health Professionals would be unable to render assistance even if they themselves were unharmed because many of the casualties would be in areas of lethal fallout. (BMA Report — 1983)

Raymond Briggs

There is no effective antidote to acute radiation. Measures that might have marginal effects would not be available after a Nuclear War[35].

The explosion of a single nuclear bomb of the size used at Hiroshima over a major city in the United Kingdom is likely to produce so many cases of trauma and burns requiring hospital treatment that the remaining medical services in the United Kingdom would be completely overwhelmed. (BMA Report — 1983)

HEAT AND BLAST EFFECTS FROM A ONE MEGATON EXPLOSION ONE MILE ABOVE BATTERSEA POWER STATION (on a clear day)

Heat effects

Example of heat effects at various distances:-

Hyde Park:- (2 miles) Trees burn spontaneously; water in the Serpentine boils.

St Paul's Cathedral:- (3 miles) Car tyres ignite; sheet metal on buses ignites. Petrol in cars ignites.

Shepherd's Bush:- (4 miles) Furniture inside buildings ignites.

Kentish Town:- (4.5 miles) Human tissue charred to bone (temperature 1800°C).

Golder's Green:- (7 miles) Full thickness skin burns to those in open. Fatal.

Hendon:- (8.5 miles) Severe second degree burns; fatal if not treated.

Harrow:- (11 miles) Eyes: permanent damage to anyone looking at fireball.

Stanmore:- (12.5 miles) Severe sunburn.

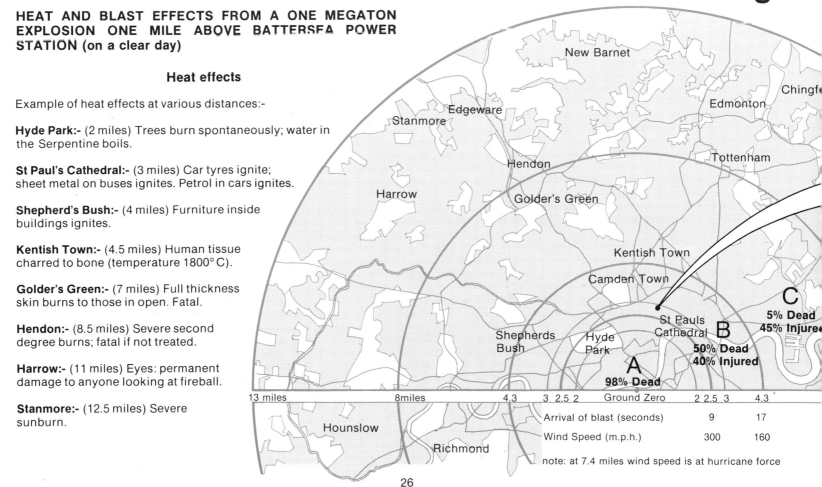

A — 98% Dead
B — 50% Dead / 40% Injured
C — 5% Dead / 45% Injured

	Ground Zero		
Arrival of blast (seconds)		9	17
Wind Speed (m.p.h.)		300	160

note: at 7.4 miles wind speed is at hurricane force

26

London

Blast effects

Zone A:- Most buildings levelled; Tower blocks fall. 98% of people in this area will die as a result of heat and blast.

Zone B:- Typical houses destroyed; Damage to heavier structures; Gas mains severed.

Camden Town:- (3.75 miles) Winds of 200 mph will result in people being thrown about at 20 mph — resulting in skull fractures in more than 50%. Also common:- compound fractures and crush injuries.

Zone C:- Walls of steel frame buildings ɔwn away; severe damage to houses. Home Office Mark I Garden Shelters destroyed.

Bethnal Green:- (5.2 miles) Injuries from penetrating glass.

Zone D:- Damage to most structures as far as Biggin Hill (13 miles south); windows blown in and roof tiles dislodged.

Ilford

D

5% Injured

Great Ormond Street Children's Hospital

Woolwich

3 miles	13 miles
35	60
68	36

Experience of a nurse looking out of a window on a clear day — from Great Ormond Street Children's Hospital

1. Flash of light three miles away resulting in permanent blindness.

2. A fraction of a second later, intense heat felt on the face and bare arms resulting in third degree (full thickness) burns, with charring down to bone.

3. Fifteen seconds later, she is dazed, semi-comatose and blind. The windows are blown in resulting in severe penetrating glass injuries.

4. A fraction of a second later, she is thrown across the ward at 50 feet per second (34 mph) by the blast and is brought to an abrupt halt on the far side of the ward as her head hits the wall: her skull is fractured.

5. As this is happening, the hospital building partially collapses. The Nurse is pinned to the floor by fallen masonry, resulting in severe trauma.

Lying in State

The recently published report on the medical effects of nuclear war by the British Medical Association (BMA) Board of Science & Education states that

There are discrepancies between the projections for blast, heat and radiation produced by the Home Office and Scientists Against Nuclear Arms (SANA). The latter rely on methods and figures derived for the most part from the United States Department of Defense and the Office of Technology Assessment. We have examined the methods for calculating the projections used by SANA and the Working Party believes, on the evidence it has received, that the projections from SANA give a more realistic estimate of the blast, heat and radiation effects of nuclear weapons. We understand that the Home Office is currently revising its calculations.

The next few pages illustrate the way the Home Office have underestimated the casualties resulting from a nuclear explosion and raises the question as to whether these discrepancies are the result of incompetence or are part of a deliberate process of deception.

Burn casualties ignored:

In a nuclear explosion one-third of the energy is released as heat and consequently there will be a considerable number of burns casualties.

The current Home Office computer model for casualty predictions makes no estimate at all for burns casualties[36][37], even though the Department of Health & Social Services (DHSS) expect "vast numbers of burns casualties"[38]. These calculations are difficult because thermal effects are dependent on weather, time of year, and number of people caught out in the open at the time of the explosion[39]. However the American Office of Technology Assessment has derived estimates of burns casualties under a variety of different conditions[40], and the same approach has been used in the Oppenshaw & Steadman computer model used by SANA[41].

Blast casualties underestimated:

There are large discrepancies between Home Office and American figures for blast casualties which are illustrated opposite.

The Home Office use casualty figures arising from CONVENTIONAL explosions while the Americans have based theirs on NUCLEAR explosions.

Following an explosion blast damage to buildings depends primarily upon two factors:-
1) The peak overpressure (measured in p.s.i.)
2) The duration of the overpressure.

In a nuclear explosion the overpressure lasts much longer (1-2 seconds) than in a conventional explosion (a few one hundredths of a second)[39]. Consequently, for the same peak overpressure a nuclear explosion will cause more destruction and loss of life than a conventional one, as was well illustrated in World War II. During the Blitz, about 70,000 tons of TNT were dropped killing approximately 60,000 people i.e. about one person killed per ton of explosive.

The two atomic bombs dropped on Japan were equivalent to 30,000 tons of TNT and killed between 100,000 and 200,000 people[10] i.e. about three to six people killed per ton of explosive (TNT equivalent).

The Home Office estimates for blast casualties in a nuclear explosion use figures arising from conventional explosions in World War II[42]. In contrast, the US Office of Technology Assessment (OTA), obtained their estimates, which they consider conservative, from data based on the Japanese experience and the atmospheric testing of nuclear weapons before the Partial Test Ban Treaty of 1963.

Blast ranges:

Blast Range is the distance from a nuclear explosion subjected to a given peak overpressure. The Home Office, in their computer model use U.S. data from Glasstone and Dolan (The Effects of Nuclear Weapons)[37].

In Home Office publications there are errors and inconsistencies for quoted blast ranges [43] [44]. These errors all result in the blast damage areas being smaller than they should be; for air bursts they have reduced blast damage areas by as much as 40%. (Page 60 ref. 1).

In addition, the "Weapon Effects Calculators" issued by the Home Office to Scientific Advisers have built-in errors. This results in the blast ranges, for higher overpressures, being smaller than those given in Glasstone and Dolan — as shown in the illustration opposite.

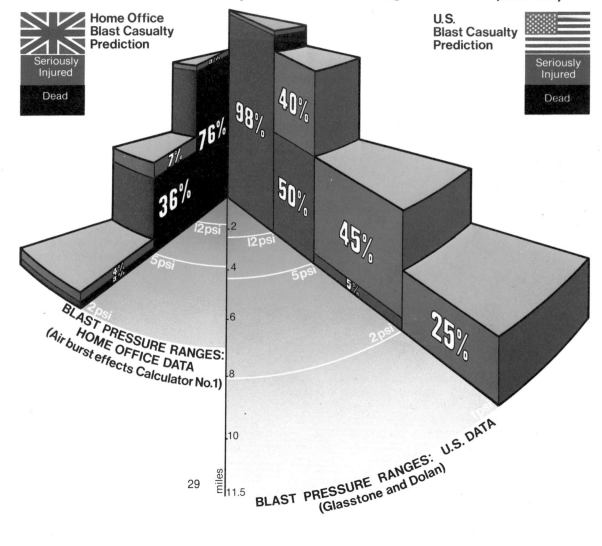

Discrepancies in Blast Casualty Predictions for a 1 Megaton Air Burst (7800 feet)

Home Office Blast Casualty Prediction

Seriously Injured

Dead

U.S. Blast Casualty Prediction

Seriously Injured

Dead

98%
76%
7%
40%
36%
50%
45%
4%
3%
5%
25%

12psi
5psi
2psi

BLAST PRESSURE RANGES: HOME OFFICE DATA (Air burst effects Calculator No.1)

BLAST PRESSURE RANGES: U.S. DATA (Glasstone and Dolan)

miles
2
4
6
8
10
11.5

29

Fallout casualties underestimated

The Home Office has underestimated casualties from fallout by overestimating the protective factor of buildings, ignoring the effect of blast damage and by underestimating the lethality of radiation.

Misleading protective factors

The protection that an individual has against fallout radiation will depend on the thickness and density of material between that individual and the radiation source, and is known as the PROTECTIVE FACTOR (PF). This is the ratio between the radiation outside the building or shelter and the radiation that penetrates inside. The higher the value the greater protection from radiation. For example PF2 means that only half (½) of the radiation penetrates, while PF10 means that only one tenth (1/10) of the radiation penetrates.

> This illustration shows the effect of a 1 megaton air burst (7800 ft) followed by a blanket of fallout radiation (2,500 rads) from a nearby ground burst — a situation that occurred in many places in the 1980 Square Leg Exercise.[46][47]
> (Burn casualties have not been taken into account.)
> The blast zone reaching out to 1 psi covers an area of 415 square miles. Assuming the average UK density of 593 persons per square mile, the area would encompass ¼ of a million people or 1½ million people if it were central London.

The US Office of Technology Assessment (OTA) quote a variety of studies on Protection Factors assumed for houses and shelters in the USA[40]. For estimating fallout casualties a range of values has been used:

PF3   for the entire population assuming that no civil defence measures have been used.
PF5-6   for people remaining in their homes.
PF10-40 for people with access to proper fallout shelters.

The OTA estimate that on average the PFs would be in the range of 5 to 6. By contrast the Home Office have assigned a very high average PF of over 20 to British housing stock[45]. The very high PFs used by the Home Office for ordinary houses are based on dubious assumptions[46], one of which is that the entire population would be able to carry out the measures suggested in the HMSO civil defence pamphlet "Protect and Survive". Such measures include:
1) Bricking up windows and doors;
2) Blocking off fireplaces with sand bags;
3) Building an inner refuge.
The net result is that the Home Office estimates for fallout casualties are misleadingly low.

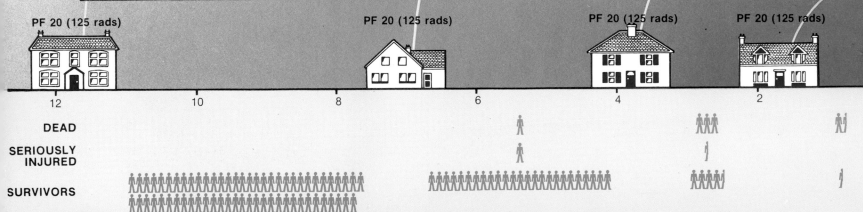

PF 20 (125 rads)   PF 20 (125 rads)   PF 20 (125 rads)   PF 20 (125 rads)

DEAD

SERIOUSLY INJURED

SURVIVORS

Blast
Radiation

CASUALTIES BASED ON HOME OFFICE ASSUMPTIONS (👤 = 1% of people in blast zone)

Blast damage ignored

Blast damage to houses reduces protection from fallout radiation. Even light blast damage such as missing roof tiles or broken windows and doors allows radioactive dust to be blown into the house greatly reducing its PF value.

The Home Office Square Leg exercise envisaged over 205 megatons being dropped on military and city targets of which about 100 megatons would be ground bursts creating local radioactive fallout[47]. Oppenshaw and Steadman calculated that in this exercise most inhabited parts of Britain experienced a blast overpressure greater than 1 psi which would break most of the windows in the country![48] Although no bomb was dropped on the centre of London in the "Square Leg" exercise, Green et al found that 75% of the GLC area was subjected to overpressures greater than 2 psi[46]. The Home Office estimates that the "Type I improvised garden shelter" would collapse under a peak overpressure greater than 1.5psi[44], so in most of London these shelters would be demolished before they could serve their intended function as fallout shelters.

Oppenshaw and Steadman using their computer model on the "Square Leg" exercise were able to estimate FALLOUT casualty figures which were dependent on the national PF value used:

PF1 (no protection)   22.5 million casualties
PF5   10.5 million casualties
PF20   3.5 million casualties

Descriptions of the Home Office computer calculations make no reference to the effect of blast damage on PF values and it appears that this relationship is ignored[36] [37]. This is illustrated by the Home Office casualty prediction of less than one million deaths for a nuclear attack, similar to the Square Leg exercise, involving 193 megatons on military and city targets of which 109 megatons were ground bursts producing the local fallout[36]. To obtain this mortality rate they must have used a PF greater than 20 which is the PF for undamaged houses.

The American figures indicate that more realistic PFs would be between 3 and 6. This would result in 8 to 10 million deaths from fallout and is a far cry from the Home Office estimate of "under 1 million".

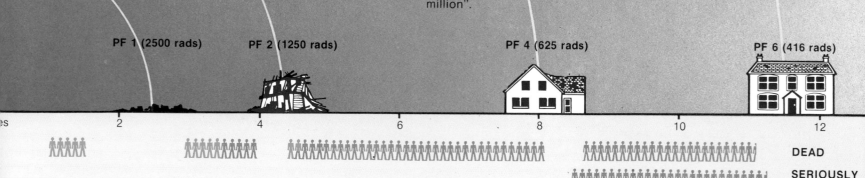

CASUALTIES BASED ON US DATA (👤 = 1% of people in blast zone)

PF 1 (2500 rads)   PF 2 (1250 rads)   PF 4 (625 rads)   PF 6 (416 rads)

DEAD
SERIOUSLY INJURED
SURVIVORS

Blast
Radiation

2 psi   1 psi

Lethality of radiation underestimated

The Home Office have also underestimated casualties by mis-application of data concerning the lethality of radiation.

Definitions: Unit of radiation = rad
LD50 = lethal dose for 50% of people
LD50 for healthy adults = 450 rads

Thus if a group of 100 healthy adults are exposed to 450 rads over a short period of time (less than one day), 50 will die even with intensive hospital treatment. (See box) The LD50 is less for children (with their smaller bodies) and old people.

Operational evaluation dose (OED)

In order to calculate operational radiation exposure limits for civil defence workers the Home Office use a formula to calculate "OED" which incorporates two pieces of data[43]:
1) Healthy adults exposed to less than 150 rads will show few if any signs of radiation exposure;
2) The body can repair about 10 rads of radiation damage per day.

The formula for "OED" is:

$$OED = \text{total radiation doses} - 150 - (10t)$$
(where t = number of days after exposure)

Medical significance of OED values		
Total Dose	Symptoms/effects	OED (t=0)
0 rads	none	—150
150 rads	nausea and 'feeling ill'	0
200 rads	vomiting	+50
250 rads	diarrhoea	+100
450 rads	50% of healthy adults die (LD 50)	+300
600 rads	chances of survival limited	+450
800 rads	90 to 100% of healthy adults die	+650

First misapplication of OED by Home Office

When it comes to calculating civilian fallout casualties the Home Office quote the LD 50 as 450 rads, in agreement with other sources. However it has recently been revealed that the Home Office in their computer model DO NOT USE 450 rads AS THE LD50; instead they equate the LD50 with an OED value of 450 which represents a dose of 600 rads i.e. 150 rads greater than the LD50[37]. This appears to be a fraudulent application of the OED expression.

Second misapplication of the OED by the Home Office

At the request of the Home Office the Protection Against Ionising Radiation Committee reassessed the effects of radiation exposure. Their informal advice to the Home Office suggested that humans are much more resistant to radiation exposure than had previously been thought. This advice, which the Home Office accepted, was:

1) The threshold below which no ill effects from radiation are expected should be increased from 150 to 200 rads.
2) That the amount of radiation that the body can repair per day should be increased from 10 to 15 rads.
3) That the LD50, the dose at which 50% of people are expected to die, should be increased from 450 to 600 rads.

The basis for this advice has not been published. (Page 84 ref. 1). Using these new figures the final row of the table opposite becomes:

Total dose		OED
600 rads	chances of survival limited	+400
800 rads	90 to 100% of healthy adults die	+600

From this it is clear that an LD50 of 600 rads is equivalent to an OED value of 400. However the Home Office again misapply the LD50 and equate it with an OED value of 600 which is equivalent to a dose of 800 rads.

Radiation Dose – Short Exposure To Whole Body

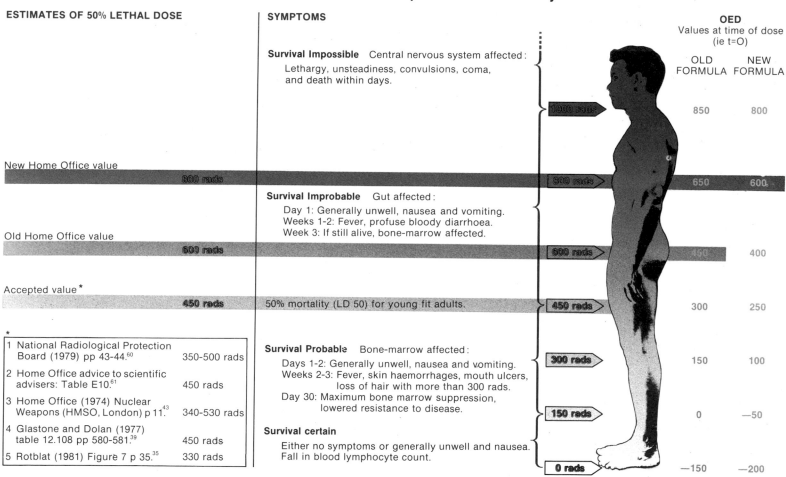

ESTIMATES OF 50% LETHAL DOSE

New Home Office value — 800 rads

Old Home Office value — 600 rads

Accepted value* — 450 rads

*
1 National Radiological Protection Board (1979) pp 43-44.[60]	350-500 rads
2 Home Office advice to scientific advisers: Table E10.[61]	450 rads
3 Home Office (1974) Nuclear Weapons (HMSO, London) p 11.[43]	340-530 rads
4 Glastone and Dolan (1977) table 12.108 pp 580-581.[39]	450 rads
5 Rotblat (1981) Figure 7 p 35.[35]	330 rads

SYMPTOMS

Survival Impossible   Central nervous system affected:
Lethargy, unsteadiness, convulsions, coma, and death within days.

Survival Improbable   Gut affected:
Day 1: Generally unwell, nausea and vomiting.
Weeks 1-2: Fever, profuse bloody diarrhoea.
Week 3: If still alive, bone-marrow affected.

50% mortality (LD 50) for young fit adults.

Survival Probable   Bone-marrow affected:
Days 1-2: Generally unwell, nausea and vomiting.
Weeks 2-3: Fever, skin haemorrhages, mouth ulcers, loss of hair with more than 300 rads.
Day 30: Maximum bone marrow suppression, lowered resistance to disease.

Survival certain
Either no symptoms or generally unwell and nausea.
Fall in blood lymphocyte count.

Dose markers: 1000 rads, 800 rads, 600 rads, 450 rads, 300 rads, 150 rads, 0 rads

OED
Values at time of dose
(ie t=O)

OLD FORMULA	NEW FORMULA
850	800
650	600
450	400
300	250
150	100
0	−50
−150	−200

Square Leg

"Square Leg" was the name given to the 1980 Home Defence exercise. The envisaged attack was 131 warheads (62 air bursts and 69 ground bursts) totalling 205 megatons on a mixture of military and city targets.

1979 Population of Britain: 54 million (each figure = 1 million)

Predicted Casualties based on

Home Office assumption ──────────────┬────────────── Openshaw/Steadman assumption

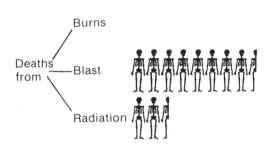

Deaths from
- Burns
- Blast
- Radiation

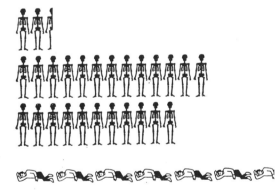

Seriously injured

Survivors

34

Square Leg

After several weeks of mounting tension, war was declared. Four days later, on Thursday 19th September 1980 at 11.55 a.m. 'Attack Warning Red' was given. Nine minutes later the first wave of bombs fell on Britain hitting strategic and industrial targets. Square Leg, the 1980 Civil Defence exercise, was in full swing[47]. Three hours after the initial attack a second wave of bombs arrived hitting targets of which many were cities. For some reason London itself was not a target although it would have suffered considerable damage from bombs that landed on the outskirts[46].

Targets chosen in the exercise seemed realistic in that many of them, though relatively unknown, were strategically important. Such targets included the two electronic listening posts at Chicksands (USAF) and RAF Digby; the two very low frequency radio stations at Rugby and Criggon, used for communicating with submerged submarines; and the US underwater monitoring post at Brawdy.

A large proportion of the strategic targets in the exercise were US bases which is not surprising as there are over one hundred such bases in Britain[63]. The official figure given for the number of US bases in Britain is 56. However, this figure was only arrived at after a series of parliamentary questions which began with the admission of 12 bases plus a 'few other facilities'[64]. When the 'few other facilities' were listed, the figure rose to 53[65]; and then to 56 when asked if the list was complete[66].

There were two noteable features of the attack. The first was underwater explosions in the Thames and Clyde estuaries producing tidal waves which would have flooded London and Glasgow. The other feature was the attack on four nuclear reactors at Dungeness and Dounreay and the nuclear waste reprocessing plant, Windscale (renamed Sellafield). The destruction of these nuclear installations, particularly Windscale, would have resulted in the release of large amounts of long lived radioactive material, increasing considerably not only the area of lethal radioactive fallout but also the time taken for the fallout to decay[62].

Planning to Survive

When contemplating the consequences of a nuclear attack on Britain one can, perhaps, forgive civil defence planners for thinking in terms of an evolutionary bottleneck from which only the 'fittest' will survive. Certainly this is the flavour of the North East Thames Health Authority War Plan which states:

If all the trees and much of the brushwood are felled, a forest may not regenerate for centuries. If a sufficient number of the great trees is left, however, if felling is to some extent selective and controlled, recovery is swift. In its way, a nation is like a forest and the aim of war planning is to secure the survival of the great trees . . . there will remain brushwood enough, if thirty million survivors can be so described. The planning policy is clearly elitist and is so because no wider policy is possible.

The appendix to this War Plan lists major historical disasters, from the plague of Justinian in AD 540 to Hulegu Khan invading Mesopotamia in 1258, in which the survival of leaders determined the survival of nations. The list is followed by the observation that:

We have warning now of the modern equivalent of plague. That is why isolation points (bunkers) *have already been equipped.*

In the background notes to the 1980 Square Leg exercise, Her Majesty's Government requested that the nation's art treasures be moved to places of safety. Two days before the expected attack the 'great trees' also moved to their bunkers.

Hard Luck, Hard Rock

Considerable public alarm arose when details of the 1980 civil defence exercise Square Leg were published in the *New Statesman*[47]. In general, the sheer scale of a nuclear attack on Britain envisaged by the Home Office, had not been appreciated.

Anticipating the inevitable publicity both the Home Office and SANA presented target plans for the 1982 civil defence exercise with code names of Hard Rock and Hard Luck respectively.

Predicted Casualties based on

Hard Rock	Hard Luck
Home Office assumption	Openshaw/Steadman assumption

Hard Rock

Hard Rock was to be the largest civil defence exercise since 1958, but was cancelled because one third of the Local Authorities refused to take part. In the past the Home Office have stressed that target plans for civil defence exercises "should not be taken as realistic descriptions . . . of the weight or distribution of an enemy's attack":[38] Hard Rock seems to be a case in point.

The attack (54 bombs with a total of 48 megatons) was puny compared with previous exercises such as Square Leg (131 bombs; with a total of 205 megatons). In addition, contrary to the recent technological advances in delivering nuclear warheads with a high degree of accuracy (500 metres and less), over half the bombs in the planned exercise missed their intended targets by 6 to 10 miles. Fortunately, most of those targets missed were cities. Some targets that did receive direct hits such as the top of Mount Carneddau had no military, industrial or civilian significance as far as we know.[38]

Hard Luck

The attack constructed by SANA was based on known Soviet Eurostrategic weapons. Those weapons, thought to be aimed at Britain, were assigned actual targets[52].

The targets selected were principally military and strategic ones, with a few urban areas included because of their industrial significance.

The attack (362 bombs with an average yield of 0.6 Mt — making a total of 222 megatons) can be seen as limited in two senses:

1) Major population centres were not deliberately targeted for their own sake.
2) Since the Soviets already possess significant weapons to direct more than 600 megatons on such an important target as the UK, the attack did not employ all the weapons that would be available.

It is interesting that the principal criticism of Hard Luck by the Home Office was that an attack of 222 megatons was excessively large, when they themselves used 205 megatons in Square Leg (1980), and indeed, have considered "worst case" scenarios involving 500 and 3000 megatons[36].

Lying in state: Post Mortem

It is difficult to conclude that errors in the Home Office casualty model when taken together are not a deliberate attempt to minimise the perceived consequences of a nuclear attack.

Although the reasons for these discrepancies are known only to those who constructed the model (members of the Home Office F6 Division), we suggest a possible motive.

The development of nuclear ballistic missiles by both the United States and the Soviet Union brought about the realisation that little could be done to protect civilian populations from the effects of a nuclear attack. Consequently, in 1968 civil defence plans in Britain were shelved. The decision was in keeping with the current idea that since both sides knew that they would be destroyed in a nuclear war, the possession of nuclear weapons guaranteed the peace.

However, with the deployment of new counterforce weapons, the risk of nuclear war has been increasing (pp 16-17).

It is, perhaps, in recognition of these changes in nuclear strategy that the Home Office have revived civil defence planning.

Certainly, the most recent civil defence exercises reflect the changes away from purely civilian targets to civilian/military ones (see table). The inclusion of military targets greatly increases the weight of attack.

Civil Defence Exercises	Number of Bombs	Total Megatons	Target
Plans for MAD strategy:			
Dutch Treat 1957	8	8	Cities
Exercise 1960	15	56	Cities
Changes to plans for counterforce strategy:			
Inside right 1976	?	?	?
Scrum half 1978	130	200	Military/Civilian
Square Leg 1980	131	205	Military/Civilian
Adverse publicity			
Hard Rock 1982	54	48	Military/Civilian

As was appreciated in the 60's, little can be done to protect civilian populations from the effects of nuclear attack. Home Office plans, therefore, concentrate on the survival of some form of regional authority (by means of shelter in deep bunkers) to be ready to organise the survivors in the post-holocaust Britain. Because of this, for the purpose of civil defence planning, casualty predictions are irrelevant, although they do have considerable impact on the public's opinion with regard to Britain's nuclear defence policies. So Home Office figures which give an optimistic impression of the consequences of a nuclear attack are useful in terms of manipulating public feeling.

A Home Office circular (E53/73) suggests that for planning purposes in the event of a nuclear attack, a survival rate of 60% can be assumed for the worst affected areas and 95% survival in other areas.

In another example quoted by Duncan Campbell[38], Sir Leslie Mavor and other Home Office staff presented a paper at a NATO conference in 1977, entitled "Post Strike Scene: UK". This paper gives, after a 180 megaton attack, an immediate survival rate of between 75-85 per cent; but after a year the survival rate dropped to between 30 and 50 percent.

In 1980 Lord Belstead used these figures in a public speech. Now the 75 per cent survival figure has stuck in people's minds, as it is often quoted by government home defence lobbyists as well as being used for local authority planning purposes.

The obsessive secrecy by the Home Office about civil defence matters has allowed the basis upon which they predict casualty figures to go unchallenged for some considerable time. This secrecy in the long run, is counter productive as it encourages a loss of confidence in the process of government as a whole.

The main cricitism of civil defence in a nuclear age is that it distracts attention away from the real problem of how do we prevent a nuclear war from ever happening.

European Security

The SS20 and Pershing II are both ballistic missiles and part of their flight goes outside the earth's atmosphere. By contrast, the Cruise Missile (Ground Launched Cruise Missile — G.L.C.M.) is effectively a pilotless aircraft with a (nuclear) warhead. Although it flies at a sub-sonic speed it is difficult to detect — partly because it flies very low over the earth's surface.

During the 1960's intermediate and short range missiles were deployed within Europe. The Soviet Union's missiles were mainly land based (e.g. SS4 & SS5). The West relied more on submarine systems (e.g. Polaris) and less on the ground-based systems such as the Pershing I.

In 1976 the USSR began to deploy the SS20, a missile with three warheads. This was eventually to replace the SS4 & SS5 which had become vulnerable to American missiles[53]. By Easter, 1983, 351 SS20's had been deployed (but not all of these were assigned for Europe). These are mobile ground launched missiles with a range of 5000 kilometres, and the West does not have any directly comparable weapons. According to the Pentagon, the balance of European forces was:-

WEST		EAST	
Delivery System	Warheads	Delivery System	Warheads
0	0	SS20 — 351	1053

Hence President Reagan's call for a Zero Option; in this, the Soviet Union was asked to remove all her SS20's and in reply the USA would not deploy any Pershing II or Cruise Missiles in Europe. But as stated above, the West has relied on other, non land-based, systems. If these other systems are brought in, the balance looks different:-

systems and warheads assigned specifically for Europe

WEST		EAST	
Delivery systems	Warheads	Delivery systems	Warheads
875	1564	2030	2798

for breakdown of figures, see page 40

Even these figures, which are taken from the International Institute of Strategic Studies Military Balance 1981-82 (with minor adjustments — see page 40) do not take into account all the systems that could be used. If all European systems are taken into account, the balance becomes:-

all systems and warheads which could be used in Europe

WEST		EAST	
Delivery systems	Warheads	Delivery systems	Warheads
6727	8157	8351	3661

The situation is further complicated by the fact that long range, inter-continental missiles of both superpowers could be, and probably are, targeted on Europe. In any event, Both East and West have the ability to devastate each other whatever the arguments may be regarding the total number of warheads. Effective parity therefore exists already; once a human being is killed once, the ability to kill him twenty times over becomes irrelevant.

The debate regarding the deployment of Cruise and Pershing II is complex; but as argued above, effective parity already exists. *What, then, is the purpose of these new weapons?*

Nuclear Weapons assigned specifically for Europe (long & medium range systems)

WEST		warheads	EAST		warheads
1. Land based missiles			SS4 & SS5		380
SSBS S3 (France)		18	SS20	(230 × 3)	690
Pershing 1A		<u>180</u>	others		<u>505</u>
		198			1575
2. Submarine based missiles					
Poseidon C3	(40 × 10)	400	SS-N-5		57
Polaris A3 (UK)	(64 × 3)	192			
MSBS—M20 (France)		80			
		672			57
3. Nuclear capable aircraft			Tu 22/M26 Backfire		104
Vulcan/Buccaneer/Jaguar (UK)		214	Tu 16 Badger		248
Mirage 1VA/111E/Super		60	Tu 22 Binder		99
Etendard France			others		715
others (eg FB11)		<u>420</u>			
		694			1166
TOTAL		1564	TOTAL		2798

Modifications:
SS20:—numbers updated— but only those assigned to Europe included.(*BBC TV Newsnight—4.5.83.*)
Polaris:—3 warheads per missile
Poseidon:—only the 5 submarines allocated to SACEUR included

The following points may help to clarify the situation:-

1. While the SS20, Pershing II and Cruise can all be regarded as long range theatre nuclear weapons, their significance is entirely different by reasons of geography. The SS20 threatens Western Europe but not the USA and therefore cannot be regarded as a strategic weapon. However, the Pershing II and Cruise missiles threaten both Eastern Europe and the Soviet Union and are, therefore, effectively strategic weapons.

2. The NATO decision to deploy Pershing II and Cruise Missiles was based on military considerations, i.e. to have the option to strike at military targets in Eastern Europe or the Soviet Union. It was not primarily a response to the SS20 though this was used politically as the reason:

The Public Debate emphasised the SS20 to the exclusion of other arguments and weapon systems. The over-emphasis on the SS20 was perhaps inevitable because it is easier to discuss publicly the need for LRTNS (Long Range Theatre Nuclear Systems) modernisation by pointing to visible Soviet capabilities than by explaining the somewhat esoteric NATO doctrine. However, while understandable, this emphasis has contributed to some of the current ambiguity concerning the precise objectives of the NATO decision. [54]

3. The SS20 is not particularly accurate (CEP 400 metres). However, both the Pershing II and Cruise are exceptionally accurate (CEP 40/50 metres) and so have the ability to destroy hardened military targets. The Pershing II is particularly suited to destroying missiles in their silos. The Cruise is not so useful in destroying such "time urgent" targets — but is highly suitable for destroying other hardened military installations[55].

4. The Pershing II and Cruise are both ground launched systems and both have a limited range. They were clearly not, therefore, intended for deployment within America. Since development of both these systems started in the 1970's it seems reasonable to assume that the US Military envisaged a role for them in Europe.

5. De Gaulle did not believe in the so-called nuclear umbrella of the USA protecting Europe. He had argued that no US President would sacrifice Chicago for Paris. Since that time, many politicians and others have come to share de Gaulle's view.

The firing of Pershing II and Cruise from Western Europe eastwards might be construed as an act for which the USA was responsible. The Soviet Union might be expected to answer with an attack on the United States mainland — and have said as much[56]. It would therefore seem that de Gaulle's argument still holds for Pershing II and Cruise. The firing of these weapons would be suicide for the United States and so can barely be credible.

What is the intention of the USA in agreeing to deploy these missiles on European soil?
There are two possible answers to this question:-

A. The missiles may be intended for use against targets in Eastern Europe with the hope that the ensuing nuclear war would be limited to Europe leaving both superpowers intact.

B. The missiles could be intended for military targets within the Soviet Union as part of a Counterforce Plan which would be reinforced by the strategic weapons of the United States including their 3780 air-launched Cruise missiles, some of which have already been deployed.

In this latter context, the deployment of Pershing II and Cruise could be seen as an integral part of Presidential Directive 59 (of July '80) in which President Carter formally adopted the counterforce strategy. This was, in fact, not a new idea but had first been considered by President Eisenhower's Secretary of State, Dulles in 1957 and further elaborated in 1974 by the then US Defence Secretary Schlesinger[55].

6. All Arms Limitation Agreements to date have depended upon the ability of both superpowers to verify the agreement. This has become possible with satellite surveillance. Many analysts fear that the deployment of the Cruise would be the end of verification as these missiles are easy to hide and hence difficult to detect.

Conclusion:-

These highly accurate weapon systems seem to be ideal for fighting a nuclear war but useless for deterring one. They have the ability to destroy the other side's military installations a short time after firing. Hence, even if a "Launch on Warning" policy is technically not feasible at present, in times of crisis there would inevitably be great pressures on both sides to fire their systems first — for to wait could result in one's own missiles being destroyed. This inevitably leads to the conclusion that the deployment of the Pershing II and Cruise missiles will reduce European security by making nuclear war more, and not less, likely.

Possiblities for reducing tension:-

The USSR has repeatedly said that it would not be the first to use nuclear weapons. Field Marshal Lord Carver and others have recently advocated that NATO should also adopt such a "No First Use" policy. While this might involve extra expenditure as a result of a necessary expansion in conventional forces, there is good evidence to suggest that such a policy would raise the nuclear threshold[57] and so reduce the risk of nuclear war.

The Arms Race over the last 30 years has followed a predictable pattern. The deployment of any new system by one superpower has resulted in the other superpower subsequently deploying a similar or comparable system — without either side becoming more secure. This would seem to be the inevitable result if the Pershing II and Cruise are deployed.

A total freeze on the deployment of all new nuclear weapon systems would overcome this danger — and at the same time remove the notion that the United States will only negotiate from a position of strength. An absurd proposition as it implies that the Soviet Union will agree to negotiate from an inferior position.

Perceptions and Morality

The extermination of Jews by the Nazi Regime still causes public outrage. Yet we seem to be blinded by the fact that the use of nuclear weapons would result in the same kind of extermination of civilian populations. One reason for this is that during the 1950's when the doctrine of Mutually Assured Destruction was evolving, few thought about the morality of these policies as they understood and believed that nuclear deterrence would not fail, and so the question of annihilating millions was not seriously considered. But this question can no longer be dismissed since the new "crisis unstable" weapons are threatening the stability which was thought to ensue from a nuclear deterrent. (See pp 12-21)

One of the main stumbling blocks in attempting to reverse the Arms Race is the ingrained attitude that each side has of the other. Both sides perceive themselves as "peacemakers" and regard their own weapons as "good" and essential — solely for defence. The other side's weapons are perceived as bad, threatening, and excessive for purely defensive requirements.

In order to justify the possession and threatened use of nuclear weapons, it becomes necessary to perceive the enemy as totally bad or evil. As the Physicist P. M. S. Blacket said some years ago:

Once a nation bases its security on an absolute weapon, such as the Atom Bomb, it becomes psychologically necessary to believe in an absolute enemy.[58]

This may well be at a subconscious level. Clearly, no nation can be absolutely evil.

Britain's nuclear deterrence can only be regarded as credible if it is assumed that in the last resort it would be used. Therefore, to accept such a policy is to accept a situation in which, if all else fails, our Government, on our behalf, would be responsible for annihilating tens of millions of Soviet Citizens — and destroying Europe in the aftermath. Such a policy would appear to be both irrational and morally unjustifiable.

The Individual's Response

The political apathy of people in time of peace indicates that they will readily allow themselves to be led to slaughter later. Because today they lack even the courage to give their signature in support of disarmament, they will be compelled to shed their blood tomorrow.
Albert Einstein.

The hopes and aspirations of human beings throughout the world are in many respects very similar, but these are becoming overshadowed by the threat of nuclear annihilation. Our feeling of helplessness caused by this can easily result in us ignoring the problem; but this will lead to catastrophe as Einstein warns. If, however, we critically study the causes and likely effects of the nuclear arms race we can, within a fairly short space of time, become more knowledgeable than many politicians in this matter. This knowledge may lead us to realise that many, while claiming to advocate disarmament, are set on an unprecedented escalation of the arms race as a result of ignorance or misinformation — particularly regarding Soviet nuclear capabilities.

As individuals in the West, where we can express our views relatively freely, we have a great responsibility to challenge the present policies which appear to be inappropriate and exceedingly dangerous. These issues are too crucial to be left to possibly ill-informed politicians.

I like to believe that people in the long run are going to do more to promote peace than governments. Indeed, I think that people want peace so much that one of these days governments had better get out of their way and let them have it.
Dwight Eisenhower (1959).

Conclusion: The Earth, Man and His Environment

The future of humanity can seldom have looked so uncertain as it does today. The world-wide process of industrialisation has accelerated rapidly since 1945 resulting in pollution of the atmosphere and in the loss of vast areas of the world's forests. The long-term consequences of these processes are both unpredictable and possibly irreversible, and may in the 21st century radically alter life on earth.

Since the Second World War most Third World Countries have achieved their independence, but now find themselves pawns within both the world economy and the military machinations of one or other superpower[8].(The Brandt Commission Report of 1980 warned of the destabilising effects of the poor countries getting progressively poorer, yet this Report has been largely ignored.)

Compounding all these problems is the threat of nuclear annihilation. Politicians often defend present nuclear policies by emphasising the 38 years of peace Europe has enjoyed since 1945 when the first Atom Bomb was exploded. Yet 38 years is a very short time in human history. If the nuclear policies of the last decade have been appropriate, the added arsenals of nuclear weapons should have made the world a safer place now compared with 1970; however, most Europeans feel less secure.

Furthermore, if it is rational for Britain to base her security on a nuclear deterrent, it is logical that other countries should also adopt such a policy. Few analysts, however, feel that world security will be increased by such horizontal proliferation of nuclear weapons.

During the last decade, Arms Limitation Talks have dragged on and on and yet the Arms Race continues. In December, 1982, the United Nations General Assembly voted by a large majority in favour of various disarmament resolutions including one on a freeze of the deployment of all new nuclear weapons. (The USA and Britain voted against this[59].) Had this resolution been adopted by the superpowers it could have been the first major step towards reducing East-West tension. In the long run, it may be necessary for individual nations to accept the majority view of the United Nations on such issues. In this way national concepts of war may have to give way to the international concept of the survival of the human race.

These problems facing the human race are not insoluble but their solution may require a change in the very way we think. As Martin Luther King said in another context: *"We must either learn to live together as brothers or we are going to perish together as fools."*

When I grow up I want to be ALIVE..

The trauma of surviving

It is a common experience for survivors of a major catastrophe to feel a deep sense of loneliness and a profound feeling of the futility of life. The psychological trauma deadens their behaviour as though they had been mentally anaesthetised without thought, without feeling.

When the outside world regains contact with the survivors, the behavioural paralysis relaxes its grip. For it is not only the material aid in the form of water, food, clothing and medicine that assists in their recovery, but the infectious vitality of human society which strengthens their will to live.

In a nuclear war there will be no regained contact, no surrounding human community, no world out there to count on. The survivors would remain in a deadened state, either alone or among others like themselves, largely without hope and vaguely aware that everyone and everything that once mattered to them had been destroyed. Thus survivors would experience not only the most extreme forms of individual trauma imaginable, but an equally severe form of collective trauma stemming from a rupture of the patterns of social existence.

Under these conditions, such simple tasks as acquiring food and maintaining shelter would remain formidable for weeks and months, even years. The band of survivors would be further reduced, not only by starvation, but also by continuing exposure to radiation and by disease.

The question so often asked: "Would the survivors envy the dead?" may turn out to have a simple answer. No, they would be incapable of such feeling. They would not so much envy as inwardly and outwardly resemble the dead.

Extracted from "Last Aid"[49] R. J. Lifton and K. Erikson.

References

1 *The Medical Effects of Nuclear War: The Report of the British Medical Association's Board of Science and Education.* John Wiley & Sons, 1983.
2 Clausewitz. *On War.* Penguin Classics.
3 Field Marshal Lord Carver: *A Policy For Peace.* Faber & Faber, 1982.
4 Herington, *John: Air Power Over Europe 1944-45.* Canberra: Australian War Memorial 1963.
5 Prins, Gwyn (Ed): *Defended to Death*, Table 1, p. 50, Pelican, 1983.
6 Tromp, H. W., La Rocque, G. R. (Eds): *Nuclear War In Europe 1982/1*, Groningen University Press.
7 Chivian, E., Chivian, S., Lifton, R. J., Mack, J. E. (Eds): *Last Aid, The Medical Dimensions of Nuclear War.* 1981, W. H. Freeman & Co.
8 Protection Civile, Federal Office for Civil Defence, Bern Switzerland.
9 Sivard, Leger, Ruth: *World Military and Social Expenditure* 1982. WMSE Publication C/o CAAT, 5 Caledonian Road, London N1 9OX.
10 *Hiroshima and Nagasaki: The Physical, Medical and Social Effects of the Atomic Bombings.* Hutchinson & Co., 1981.
11 Forsberg, R.: 'A Bilaterial Nuclear Weapon Freeze', *Scientific American*, November er 1982, Vol. 247.
12 *SPRI Year Book 1980.* Taylor & Francis.
13 *World Population Trends and Policies, 1977 Monitoring Report, Vol 1, Population Trends,* UN; New York, 1979.
14 Source quoted from *Defended to Death*, Editor Gwyn Prins, Pelican 1983. R. McNamara, Annual statement to the Senate Armed Services committee, 1 February 1968, reproduced in *Survival*, April 1968, pp. 106-114 (modified) from D. T. Johnson and B. R. Schneider *Current Issues in US Defense Policy*, New York 1976 p. 142.
15 Openshaw, S. and Steadman, P: 'On the geography of a Worst Case Nuclear Attack on the Population of Britain', *Political Geography Quarterly*, 1982; 3 pp. 263-278.
16 Aldridge, R. C.: *The Counterforce Syndrome: A Guide to U.S. Nuclear Weapons and Strategic Doctrine',* 1978, Institute for Policy Studies (obtained from Pluto Press).
17 Tsipis, K.: *Offensive Missiles, SIPRI* Stockholm Paper 1974, p. 16.
18 Prins, Gwyn (Ed): *Defended to Death*, Pelican, 1983, p. 299.
19 *SIPRI Yearbook 1980.* Taylor & Francis.

20 *Soviet Military Power*, 2nd Edition 1983 US Department of Defense, US Govt. Printing Office, Washington DC.
21 *Counterforce Issues for the US Strategic Nuclear Forces,* Congressional Budget Office Background Paper, January 1978, p. 32.
22 *Defence in the 1980's: Statement on the Defence Estimate*, HMSO London April 1980, p. 15. para. 212.
23 *SIPRI Yearbook 1981*, chap. 2. 'The Evolution of Military Technology and Deterrence Strategy'. Taylor & Francis Ltd.
24 *Defence in the 1980's, Statement on the defence Estimate* HMSO London April 1980, p. 18, para. 307.

25 *SIPRI Yearbook, 1981*, p. 10. Taylor Francis Ltd.
26 Halloran, R. 'Pentagon draws up first strategy for fighting a long nuclear war', *New York Times*, 29 May 1982.
27 Fairhall, D.: Strategies of the strong arm men, *Guardian* 3rd May 1983, p. 19.
28 Churchill, Winston S.: *The Second World War,1* 'The Gathering Storm'.
29 Prins, Gwyn: *Defended to Death*, Pelican 1983 Chapter 5, 'The Steel Triangle'.
30 Geiger, H. Jack: 'The Medical Effects on a City in the United States'. *Last Aid — The Medical Dimensions of Nuclear War.* W. H. Freeman and Co. 1981.
31 Abrams, Herbert L. 'Survivors of Nuclear War: Infection and the Spread of Disease'. ibid.
32 *World Health.* The magazine of World Health Organisation, May 1980, p. 18.
33 Briggs, Raymond: *When the Wind Blows.* Hamish Hamilton Ltd. 1981.
34 Crutzen, Paul J. & Birks, John W.: 'The Atmosphere After a Nuclear War: Twilight at Noon'. *Ambio — A Journal of the Human Environment* Vol. XI; No. 2-3; 1982.
35 Rotblat, J.: *Nuclear Radiation in Warfare*, SIPRI, Taylor and Francis 1981.
36 Butler, S. F. J., 'Scientific advice in Home Defence' in Barnaby, C. F. and Thomas G. P. (Eds), *The Nuclear Arms Race: Control or Catastrophe* 1982 Frances Pinter, London pp. 135-163.
37 Bentley, P. R. *Blast overpressure and fallout radiation dose models for casualty assessment and other purposes.* Home Office Scientific Research and Development Branch report 1981.
38 Campbell, D: *War Plan UK: The Truth about Civil Defence in Britain*, p. 135 Burnett Books, London 1982.
39 Glasstone S. and Dolan P. J. (Eds): *The Effects of Nuclear Weapons* 3rd edition, Castle House, Tunbridge Wells, 1977.
40 US Office of Technology Assessment (OTA) *The Effects of Nuclear War* Croom Helm, London, 1980.
41 Openshaw, S. and Steadman, P: 'On the geography of the Bomb', paper tresented to conference of the Institute on British Geographers, Edinburgh 5 January 1983.
42 Home Office, 'The control of civil defence operations under fallout conditions' *Civil Defence Training Memorandum No. 3* HMSO, London, 1959.
43 Home Office, *Nuclear Weapons* HMSO, London, 1974.
44 Home Office,, *Domestic Nuclear Shelters: Technical Guidance* HMSO, London, 1981.
45 Home Office, *Fission Fragments* No. 31 June 1982 Home Office (in-house magazine).
46 Greene, O., Rubin, B., Turok, N., Webber, P and Wilkinson, G.: *London After The Bomb: What a nuclear Attack really means*, Oxford University Press 1982.
47 Campbell, D: World War III: an exclusive preview, *New Statesman*, 3 October 1980. Scotland's Nuclear targets *New Statesman* 6th March 1981.
48 Openshaw, S. and Steadman, P: 'Predicting the Consequences of a Nuclear Attack on Britain: Models, results and public policy implications'. *Environmental and Planning C*, in press.
49 Lifton, R. J., Erikson, K.: 'Survivors of Nuclear War: Psychological and Communal Breakdown', *Last Aid: The Medical Dimensions of Nuclear War.* W. H. Freeman & Co.

50 Fetter, S. A.and Tsipis, K.: 'Catastrophic Release of Radioactivity', *Scientific American*, April 1981.
51 Chazov, Y. I., Ilyin, L. A. and Guskova, A. K.: *The Danger of Nuclear War: Soviets Physicians viewpoint*, Novosti Press Agency Publishing House Moscow, 1982.
52 Greene, O., Steadman, P: *Doomsday: Nuclear Target Britain* in Press.
53 Holloway, David: *The Soviet Union and The Arms Race*. Yale University Press 1983.
54 *The North Atlantic Assembly Interim Report of the Special Committee on Nuclear Weapons* — Z222 CS/AW (82) 9 September '81.
55 *SIPRI Yearbook 1982*. Part I, Chapter 1. Taylor and Francis Ltd.
56 Mather, Ian: SS20 aimed at West. *Observer* 1 May 1983.
57 Field Marshal Lord Carver: *The Tablet,* 18.12.82 and 25.12.82.
58 Richter, H. E.: 'The Psychological effects of living under the threat of nuclear war' — Quoting the words of the Physicist, P. M. S. Blackett. *The Human Cost of Nuclear War* — MCANW Publication, Tenison Road, Cambridge CB1 2DG.
59 *Guardian* 15.12.82.
60 National Radiological Protection Board *The radiological consequences of notional accidental releases of radioactivity from Fast Breeder Reactors* NRPB-R-87 1979.
61 Home office advice to Scientific Advisors *Brief exposure of whole body to ionising radiation.*
62 Fetter, A. and Tsipis, K.: 'Catastrophic Releases of Radioactivity', Scientific American, April 1981.
63 Campbell, D.: Britain and the Bomb. New Statesman London 1981.
64 Hansard, 18 June 1980, col. 587.
65 Hansard, 7 July 1980, col. 54.
66 Hansard 8 August 1980, col. 481.

Recommended Books

Fearing the confusion in choice we recommend just two books:

When The Wind Blows by Raymond Briggs first published by Hamish Hamilton Ltd 1982.

Defended To Death: A study of the nuclear arms race from the Cambridge University Disarmament Seminar. Edited by Gwin Prins published by Pelican 1983.

APPENDIX — Fields of Destruction

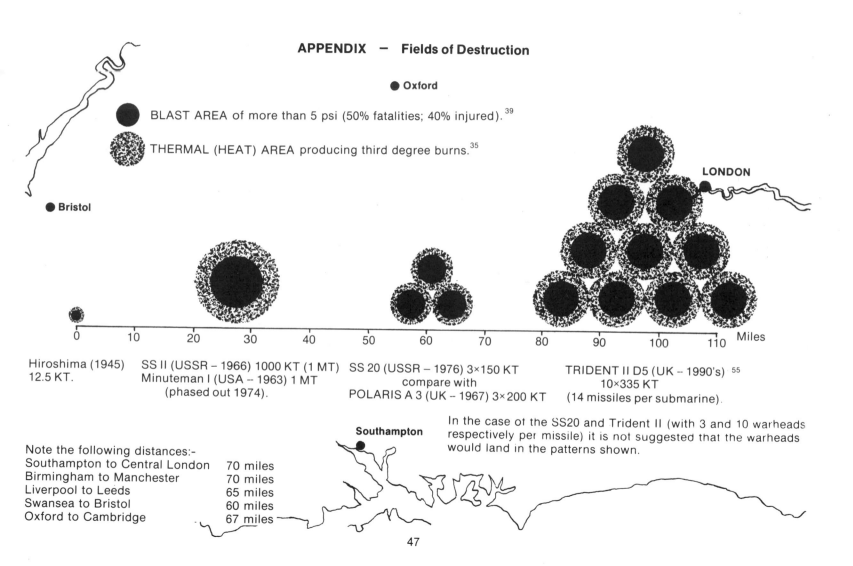

● Oxford

● BLAST AREA of more than 5 psi (50% fatalities; 40% injured).[39]

THERMAL (HEAT) AREA producing third degree burns.[35]

● Bristol

LONDON

| 0 | 10 | 20 | 30 | 40 | 50 | 60 | 70 | 80 | 90 | 100 | 110 | Miles |

Hiroshima (1945)
12.5 KT.

SS II (USSR – 1966) 1000 KT (1 MT)
Minuteman I (USA – 1963) 1 MT
(phased out 1974).

SS 20 (USSR – 1976) 3×150 KT
compare with
POLARIS A 3 (UK – 1967) 3×200 KT

TRIDENT II D5 (UK – 1990's) [55]
10×335 KT
(14 missiles per submarine).

Southampton

In the case of the SS20 and Trident II (with 3 and 10 warheads respectively per missile) it is not suggested that the warheads would land in the patterns shown.

Note the following distances:-
Southampton to Central London   70 miles
Birmingham to Manchester   70 miles
Liverpool to Leeds   65 miles
Swansea to Bristol   60 miles
Oxford to Cambridge   67 miles

47

Supernanny

How to Get the Best
from Your Children

Jo Frost

HODDER &
STOUGHTON

First published in Great Britain in 2005 by Hodder and Stoughton
A division of Hodder Headline

The moral right of the author has been asserted

A Hodder Book

10 9 8 7 6 5 4 3 2 1

A CIP catalogue record for this title is available from the British Library

ISBN 0 340 897767

Photography by Mark Read
Typeset in Century Schoolbook and News Gothic
Designed and typeset by Smith & Gilmour, London
Printed and bound by L.E.G.O. SpA, Vicenza, Italy

The publisher would like to thank all the children who appear in this
book: Thalia Cooley, Katie Cooley, Thomas Howland, Emily Howland,
Alex Hughes, Emmanuelle Martin, Tobias Sutton, Phoebe Sutton,
Daisy Sutton, Melissa De Araujo, Millie Pearson, Delta Rae Read,
Georgie Smith, Eden Soroko, Anna Soroko, Mya Williamson, Oscar Riddle,
Isaac Riddle

Hodder Headline's policy is to use papers that are natural, renewable
and recyclable products and made from wood grown in sustainable
forests. The logging and manufacturing processes are expected to
conform to the environmental regulations of the country of origin

Hodder and Stoughton Ltd
A division of Hodder Headline
338 Euston Road, London NW1 3BH

JO'S ACKNOWLEDGEMENTS

So many people have helped this book
happen. I'd love to be able to thank you
all individually but there are too many
names! Where would I begin?

So, a big, big thank you to everybody
who worked so hard on *Supernanny* at
Ricochet Productions, to the creative crew
who photographed, assisted and designed
the book and to the gang at Hodder for
delivering it.

A special thank you to the families that
made the series happen, to the families over
the years that I've worked with, and to MY
family and friends – you know who you are!
– who have supported me and then some.

And last, but not at all least, I'd like
to thank Sue Ayton and Liz Wilhide for
helping me find my voice.